# *Pain Perdu*

## *A*
## *Journey*
## *Repurposed*

*from JK Klein*

<u>*Pain Perdu*</u>

*A*

*Journey*
*Repurposed*

PPerroni Press, New Orleans, LA 70119
Copyright © 2019, by JK Klein



Email: pperronipress@gmail.com

Made in the United States of America.

"Maybe what was unusual or weird
was basically my life up till then.
Because up till then for me living
was the same as running through
hell with a gasoline suit on"

-Russel Banks-
Rule of the Bone

# Contents

*Foreword*

My involvement with "Pain Perdu"
grew partly from my own past, and revelations.
My mind wasn't ready to be open, had it been,
this book would not exist, or rather, I would cer-
tainly not be involved, as I spent decades living
life like a man attempting to mow a lawn with a
sewing machine. However, I am grateful that my
1+2 equaled 8, and I splashed ashore in New
Orleans at age 37, stumbling from the seat of a
19 hour Amtrak ride from Chicago, carrying 3
bags, one of them being defeat. I arrived from
what felt like everywhere and nowhere, briefly
dwelling inside one of many rooms within a
worn building a touch outside the French Quar-
ter. I spent several nights lying atop a mattress,
peering out a window, my head propped slightly
on a crumpled sport coat I used as a pillow.
"What am I gonna do now," I whispered to my-
self in a state of utter hopelessness.

I discovered a roommate wanted craigslist ad as I searched for a permanent living situation, met two guys, one of them being Jonathan, a talented writer, and a man who, like myself, was lost in the woods. I moved into the vacant room, and occupied myself with work, occasionally scribbling short humor pieces for magazines, and simply started my life over. Jonathan in the next room spent time writing as well, in between gulps of Skol Vodka, the bottle neatly tucked in his back pocket, as his pen hit the paper. He worked the overnight shift at a Hotel in the French Quarter, returned to the apartment around 7am, unscrewed the cap of the bottle, began writing, revising, his stomach and brain bubbling with cheap Vodka. Every Sunday, I would rise at dawn, jump into my penguin out- fit for the brunch shift, and hop the streetcar to the French Quarter. I'd sit at the bar next door to where I worked, sip my lukewarm Shell Station coffee, and chat with the overnight bartender still up from God knows when. Jonathan fre- quented that same bar after his overnight shift, sitting at the wooden counter, his head hung low, like a turtle ready to retreat into its shell.

Springtime arrived and Jonathan left the apartment, for good, a shakey, sweaty version of his true self, and I didn't know if I would ever seen him again. I managed to keep in touch periodically over the course of a year; one night I received a call, and walked across Canal Street, heading towards a park where Jonathan was living. The lights of the park illuminated the man dying of desperation. I had been there. The following day, Jonathan began his life again, and the pieces that follow are a representation of his journey; a journey of transformation leading to hope. People lose their way, and the unfortunate ones cannot, or will not, find their way back. I am grateful I found my way back, and in doing so, I was able to collaborate on this book with my friend, serving as a deal in which we both made with the environment, turning our attention to energies supporting us, ultimately discovering the journey to self-love. Thank you all for taking the time to read the words from a brilliant mind, a mind...repurposed.

--Paul Perroni,
Publisher

<u>*Acknowledgements*</u>

I want to thank my friends and family
that have shown their support, not only through
this process, but through my daily recovery.
To Paul, your encouragement and example
has shown me that my story is worth telling.
Your vision sparked the creativity I had long
abandoned, and to you, I am eternally grateful.
To Taury, for giving me what was so freely
given you, I am truly inspired to be the most
authentic version of myself, and carry that
message. For Richard, a fellow poet, I am
especially thankful. Your council and assistance
on this project has been instrumental. To my
dearest, Jamie, none of this would be possible
without you opening your home and heart to me.
I am forever changed, and cherish the life we
share.To my mother, your wellspring of prayer
and guidance through my otherwise pitiful and
incomprehensible demoralization, has prevailed,
and restored me to provenance.

—Jonathan—

# _Pain Perdu_

### A
#### _Journey_
#### _Repurposed_

*Tell my daughter*
*I'm t r y i n g*
*Have her tell my mother*
*I appreciate the guidance*
*Have her tell my father*
*I haven't di e d  ye t*
*my brother, Undecided*
*Black Smoke—still rising*
*enjoying the Si l e n ce*

Cold in december

                   seldom snow
reeds in the swamp

                     never blown
    raised
    the
    Benchmark

                I prefer I don't
showing my scars

               that's the goal
and you'll show me yours
and let the healing th  r  o    u   g  h
it's how we sing the truth
it's why I get up every day
and  e n   t   e   r      the     room

I have a new blueprint
clean to the slab of all the sentiment
Pursuit of Happiness
proving to be for the betterment
when you're asleep
I'm AWAKE Late Night
working out words
like a Letterman
I don't need no stinking badge
to cover up my fabric
of imagination, IF
there's a hole in my story
I'm—fracking it
been crude, now refined
and the gas is lit

I was a rock at the bottom
                 of the creek bed
UNSEEN when the water's frozen;

           Hoped you'd reach in,
then I'd KNOW
                 if we were in season,
                      or sequence;

                 needed

           yOU  to  fEEL

                 The

                 PAin

           enveloping ME

           In your fingers

*Am I worth the WAIT?*
    *I've been weightless*
*triple zero on the last three ex's*
  *wishing I was straight-edged*
*K-Bar on my waist*
  *to cut myself from the inside*
*hesitation*
  *how can I perform an autopsy*
*if I keep shaking,*
    *living "life by the drop"*
*like Stevie Ray did?*
    *it's gonna kill me*
*If I don't make some changes*
  *I've got to break the chains*
*of self-medication*
  *It's the only thing I've known*
*since '98-ish*

I feel the Spring
when I'm falling
though I froze
I can soften
melt unsalted
into seasoning
found in New Orleans

Escaped

with
out
Capture                raised
                       to wait for
                       rapture, so
                       I move passed
                       her

not
here
to
preach                 but
                       paSS
                       the basket

called the jew
brought up Catholic
realized I had a roman profile
started P
         a
          d
          d
           l
           i
            n
             g

*Though it hurts*
*I let go and own it—j*
          *u*
            *m*
          *p*—*in*
                *the*
                *deep-end*

*take a breath*
*blow it——And sink in* 
                    *till you*
                    *Hear me*
                    *SCREAM*

*through*
 *the*
 *bubbles*                *floating*

*even*
 *better*                *with my*
                         *Eyes*
                          *O-pen*

*So I can*
 *feel*
 *the Burn*               *of the*
                          *Moment*

MY WAY HAD TOO MANY EXITS
R    S T LE      S S
  E

DO I FILL THE TANK
OR GET SOME BREAKFAST
LIVING BETWEEN THE LINES
OF THE WEDDING AND INDEX
WANTING PROPS AND RESPECT
R  E  A  L  I  Z  E  D
THAT'S A BYPRODUCT
AIN'T NO SECRET

Got the RIGHT key!
wrong hole, You're mistaken
willing to catch a charge?
BREAK IN!
I've got some flaws
building character
looking for more lines
camera time
and syndication
PLEASE recognize
once I let you IN
you're STAYING
MY HEART,
an amusement park, mostly waiting
I've known my faults
been QUAKING
I've split myself in half
trying to balance out
self~
~hatred

IN
the
moment

won't escape it
focused on my journey
and the many stages
no invitations
it's an obligation

welcome

to

my

wake

SEE

me

waving?

The CROWDs                    are nIMbo

cumulations of Trials and Tribulations
and then some
Bells toll, wind B\LOWS
WE let go

*Passions embedded in*
*M* <sup>O</sup> *V I* <sup>N</sup> *G like etceteras*
*dot     Dot     DOT*
*ahead of me*
*My forethought—a sore spot*
*sort of negative*
*moment I put it out there*
*It's to the detriment*
*I consider it—fist to my chin*
*over Thinking IF…*

*Have a question? ASK it now!*
*Or, hear it at your commencement*
*It goes IN one ear*
*then OUT the other*
*guess the moon is waxing*
*you're gowned and capped, then*
*#hasslewithatassel*
*You're the team captain?*
*another bro-bro!*
*screaming YOLO!*
*leading me to caption*

*some——listen*

*some——read*

*depending on their senses*
*some of us can smell it*
*It's touching*
*I can taste it*
*less thinking*
*then, I won't lose*
*the FEELING*

if you like me that much
   go school yard
kick me in the shins
   i'll blow a kiss
hope someone catches it
   or pumps a fist
show them my sedative
   patience
with the narrative
   a little boy coloring
to a manuscript

Y'hear the news?
I changed my tune
got the Main Ingredient
"ain't gon' play the fool"
just so y'know you're not alone
when y'move in the opposite direction
of your compass
DEW

North

South

East

West

no matter where your feet rest
i'll be next to you
like a bride and groom...
this is OUR

H O N E Y
  O N E
M O O N
    O O

ON THE BALANCE BEAM
NO MORE SEE- SAW
REMIND RECLINE RESTART
IS HOW I GOT THIS FAR

*not stopping till i hit the station*
      *predetermined*
         *i'm a passenger*
         *i'm a traveler*

*two duffle bags*

*a backpack*

   *And*

     *my*

 *s  t  a  m  i  n  a*

I sit back like italics
        *and introspect*
      need some character building
                    in my script

   No
camera

                              No
                              film

ALWAYS point it—at me

                    never at them

Till I wrap the set—cash the SAG check
        forget the bills
        mis-directed
           SELF
          WILLED

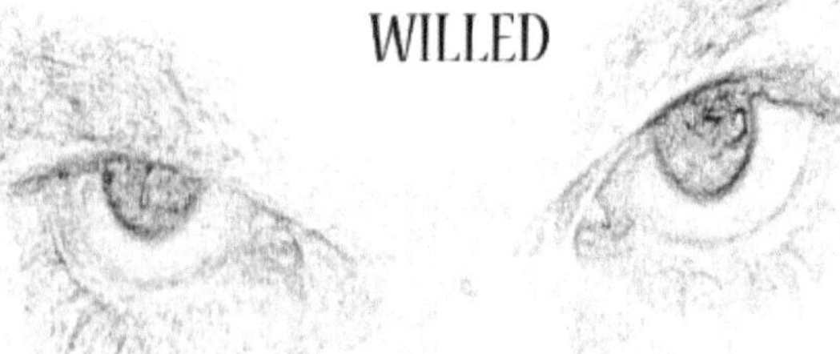

Won't lose
        had to choose
I had something to prove
            What could I do?
        It's not science
can't deny it
        there's no excuse
            climate changed
lightning came
        I Became, Who?
            If I could define it
who'd be amused?
        used to incite a fight
            so I could write
then turn the page
        black and blue

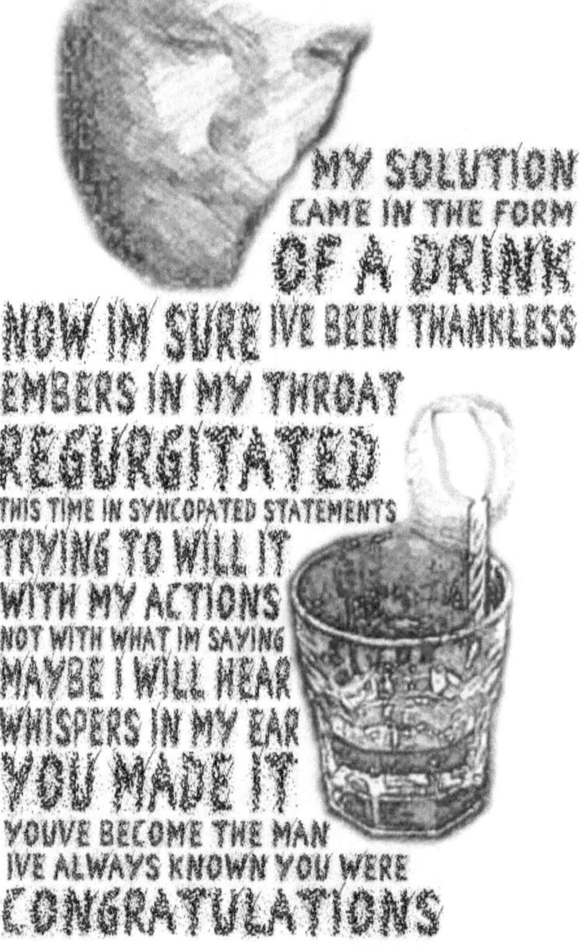
MY SOLUTION
CAME IN THE FORM
OF A DRINK
NOW IM SURE IVE BEEN THANKLESS
EMBERS IN MY THROAT
REGURGITATED
THIS TIME IN SYNCOPATED STATEMENTS
TRYING TO WILL IT
WITH MY ACTIONS
NOT WITH WHAT IM SAYING
MAYBE I WILL HEAR
WHISPERS IN MY EAR
YOU MADE IT
YOUVE BECOME THE MAN
IVE ALWAYS KNOWN YOU WERE
CONGRATULATIONS

                    to each
               their own
               whether
               Feast.
               famine.
               moved on with
               my own
               Commandments .

                              .

                    .

                       in

                              a

                       city

                              of

Lies

          "A NOLA-ANTHEM"
          haven't written that
          but i plan to

Is
it important
if you're not recording?
is it—social distortion?
Yet again...
I'm not impervious
I'm guilty of the same damn thing
I—accepted it
documented it under a bridge
No—Dif f e r   en c e

*I'm WRONG—when*
*I'm RIGHT—can't lie*
*Sometimes——feels like*
*I should ball up, and cry*
*See it in my eyes*
*Hear it in the rhyme*
*SURPRISED?*
*not afraid to admit*
*I wonder——*
*WHO AM I?*
*Am I alive?*
*I'm a student*
*of the SKY*
  *Till*
          *it*
   *ALL*
        *aligns*

My roots

grew up

Autumn

the leaves

colors

now fruit

bloomed

came

loosened

changed

produces

Both CONFUSED

Either Way

SAME as YOU!

Wont make a difference

Wont LISTEN

How OLD are you?

how old am I?

Hope WE compute

Same league Same team

Thought I had a Glossy finish BUT I'm BRICK
you know the one in the middle of the sidewalk
that I kick to the side so the next person
that walks by won't TRIP
Let's coexist

# Rose

from the ashes
without an urn
took a couple steps
toward what I deserve
Looking for a fan
was overblown
trapped in this page
so ALONE
thats why
I reach out for you
and hope one day
we share a soul
and that you know
the scars you behold
are BEAUTIFUL

" Do they stop and THINK
of what they say?"
"Who's to say they have Horns or Halos?"
"Would the subject matter change?"

*I sit, I write*
*while on a bench*
*free thoughts*
*at three in the morning*
*Or, like a dew-mist*
*cross half the nation*
*while they're in their bed*
*that's interNET*
*web entanglement*
*with —exoskeletons*

On the road to the Last House on the Block
No shade, just rain, when the sun's out
one lane, one way, headed dew South
wearing out my soul trying to out run god
kiss pain, hug shame, learned to love wrong
In a room full of windows heard a new song
"you're not alone, welcome home, grab a chair son
you're just a ship in a bottle coming unstrung"
Never open to suggestions
Was on the coast looking for a boat that won't come
No hope, No rope but still hung, up
on resentments, let my will run, riot
through the muck and mire, sirens and handcuffs
tired of the push and pull, let the tide rise, thy will done
Surprised I'm Alive, I found the Solution